To SOPHIA
You are the
GREATEST!
Love from
. . . .

D1346367

She's really the GREATEST!

Sophia is **THOUGHTFUL**,
And **HUGS** like a bear.
When you need somebody,
She'll always be there.

The FUNNIEST monkey you'll find at the zoo ...

Sophia will bring out the giggles in you!

A CURIOUS bunny,
Sophia asks more, like,
"Where did this come from?"
"What's this by the door?"

EGYPTIAN
MUMMY

BRITAIN'S
COOLEST
MUSEUM

NO HUGGING
THE EXHIBITS

She's bananas for apples
And peachy for grapes ...

Sophia loves EATING
Her food in all SHAPES!

When facing her fears,
She might find things
frightful ...

Then out ROARS
a lion,
So BRAVE and
delightful.

And even when things get
A little bit hairy,
Sophia will laugh,
"This isn't so scary."

This wise little owl's
Remarkably CLEVER,
She finds her way through
Almost any endeavour.

Sophia LOVES numbers,
And adds up with ease.
"I think I've enough
To buy five roses, please."

A real human rhino,
Sophia is STRONG –

BUS
STOP

TIMETABLE

Tower of London
Brecon Beacons
Balmoral Castle
Titanic Belfast
Ring of Kerry

Nothing's too heavy,
Too large or too long.

She NAPS like a sloth
And can snooze anywhere.

Sophia dreams BIG
Going here, going there.

Sophia's so BUSY,
She beavers along ...
HARD-WORKING
and FOCUSED,

So what could go wrong?

(And sometimes when things
Don't quite go to plan ...
We know that Sophia's tried
All that she can.)

As SWEET as a kitten
And utterly CUTE,
Sophia is LOVING
And GENEROUS to boot.

She's travelled all over,
From farms to fairs,
To show someone special
Just how much she cares.

So, there now you have it,
Sophia is best.
So FRIENDLY and FUNNY
And BRAVE ... and the rest.